The
Benghazi
Scandal

Betrayed In Benghazi

Richard S. Parker

Table Of Contents

Introduction

On the night of September 11, 2012, two separate attacks occurred at United States compounds in Benghazi, Libya that resulted in the deaths of four Americans, including Ambassador Jonathan Christopher Stevens, the first American ambassador to die in the line of duty in more than twenty years. In addition to Ambassador Stevens, Information Officer Sean Smith and embassy security guards Tyrone Woods and Glen Doherty also lost their lives in the attack.

A year after the attacks, there is much debate as to what actually happened in Benghazi. The events are in dispute and there is intense speculation that the United States government was warned about the attacks. There is a prevalent theory circulating among many reputable government officials that the U.S. State Department was involved with a weapons deal that sent armaments to mercenaries in Syria.

Although the government continues to insist that the attack was orchestrated by al-Qaeda terrorists over an anti-Islamic video that surfaced just prior to the attacks in Benghazi. The video, titled Innocence of Muslims, denounced the prophet Muhammad and resulted in outrage among Middle Eastern Islamic communities. While there were eight other attacks in the area during this time, whistle blowers believe the murder of the four Americans had nothing to do with this video.

Details are still emerging about the Benghazi incident; however, by compiling various eye-witness accounts of that night, a factual narration of what occurred has emerged and the truth may be difficult to swallow. But a blind eye cannot be turned. The government's actions before, during and after the incident speak volumes about the priorities and ambitions of this administration. Only the truth can prevent a situation such as this from happening again.

Chapter 1

Who was Ambassador Jonathan Christopher Stevens?

Jonathan Christopher Stevens was born in Grass Valley, California in 1960 to California Assistant Attorney General Jan S. Stevens and Mary J. Stevens (Floris). He had a younger sister Anne, and a younger brother Thomas. He also had half-sister, Hilary from his father's second marriage following a divorce from Mary in 1975.

Stevens graduated from Piedmont High School in 1978 after spending a year as an exchange student in Spain in 1977. He attended the University of California, Berkley, where he received a B.A. in history in 1982. He joined the Peace Corps in 1983 and taught English in Morocco. He attended the University of California, Hastings College of the Law and received a J.D. in 1989. In 2010, Stevens received an M.S. degree from the National War College.

Stevens practiced international trade law in Washington D.C. before he joined the United States Foreign Service in 1991. At that time his California Bar status was changed to inactive, and it remained that way for the rest of his career.

Stevens was assigned to Jerusalem, Damascus, Cairo and Riyadh during his stint in the United States Foreign Service. He also served as Pearson Fellow with the Senate Foreign Relations Committee, Director of the Office of Multilateral Nuclear and Security Affairs, Iran desk officer, special assistant to the Under Secretary for Political Affairs and staff assistant in the Bureau of Near Eastern Affairs.

His appointment as Ambassador in Libya in May, 2012 was his third stint in the country. He served as the Deputy Chief of Mission between 2007 and 2009 and as Special Representative to the National Transitional Council between March 2011 and November 2011.

According to his family, J. Christopher Stevens, referred to as "Chris" was passionate about building bridges between the Middle East, Africa and the United States. Several charities, programs, scholarships and initiatives have been established in Stevens' name to help promote awareness of his life's dedication to increasing communication between the United States and the Middle East.

Ambassador Stevens was pleased to have been appointed to Libya again, as is evidenced in his diary. On September 11, the day of his death, he wrote, "It's so nice to be back in Benghazi." He had just returned from a nine-month absence a few days earlier and his connection to the area was evident in the affectionate manner he used when discussing the region. It is also clear from his diary that Stevens felt like his life was in danger. His final entry in his diary grimly predicted his own death: "Never ending security threats. . ." He knew something was about to go down, which means the Obama Administration did too.

Although Ambassador Stevens was aware that he was in a dangerous situation in Benghazi, he could not have predicted the violent response to Special Operations strikes, of which he knew nothing about. The Department of Defense does not have to tell anyone about its actions, particularly when they aren't exactly above board.

Even though the White House insists that steps are being taken to ensure security breaches such as the one that eventually killed

Ambassador Stevens never happens again, it is critical to understand why it happened in the first place. This report provides a comprehensive look at the events that led up to that fateful night in Benghazi and the Obama Administration's response to Ambassador Stevens' death. Only through understanding the events of this tragic situation can similar circumstances be avoided in the future.

Chapter 2

Months in the Making

In studying the months leading up to September 11, 2012, one thing is evident: the attack on Benghazi was not a spontaneous event. There were signs all over the place that an attack was imminent. Ambassador Stevens knew it and so did everyone serving in dangerous areas in the Middle East.

In April 2012, two ex-guards for the United States consulate threw a handmade bomb over the fence surrounding the consulate. Four days later, a second bomb was tossed into a vehicle convoy, which turned out to be the United Nations Envoy to Libya. No one was injured in either attack, but they highlighted the volatility in the region.

A month later in May, 2012, a group calling itself the Imprisoned Omar Abdul Rahman Brigadeas took responsibility for an attack on the International Red Cross office located in Benghazi. This group is an off-shoot of Al-Qaeda and the incident resulted in the closing of the Red Cross office in Benghazi in August. The Red Cross delegation in Libya subsequently expressed its concern over the escalating violence in the area.

On June 5, 2012, an explosion occurred outside of the United States consulate in Benghazi. Although there were no injuries, the perimeter wall sustained major damage. The Imprisoned Omar Abdul Rahman Brigades claimed responsibility for the explosion via a video released later in the month. The group said the attack was in response to the death of an Al-Qaeda leader, Abu Yahya al Libi who had been killed in a U.S. drone attack. Although a U.S. diplomat had been scheduled to arrive on the same day as the explosion, no one was injured. However, the group warned there would be future attacks.

Five days later, on June 10, there was an assassination attempt on Dominic Asquith, the British ambassador to Libya. The ambassador was unharmed, but two British protection officers were injured when a rocket-propelled grenade hit the convoy just 300 yards from the consulate. The British Foreign Office withdrew the staff from the consulate several days later, citing safety concerns.

June 18 marked the last incident prior to the actual attack on September 11. The Tunisian consulate located in Benghazi was attacked by people connected to Ansar Al-Sharia Libya. According to reports, the attack was in retaliation to "attacks by Tunisian artists against Islam."

Early in September, a Libyan CIA informant in the region was assassinated by the United States. At that point, the Libyans were incensed because they had been assisting America by giving them subversive information only to have the informant killed by the country they were supposedly helping. This led to an assault on the State Department compound, which proved to be more successful than the militia thought it would be. It is possible the subsequent attack on the CIA compound was an additional measure of retaliation for the targeted killing of the informant.

In his diary, Ambassador Stevens wrote on September 6 that the Libyan transitional government was unstable in the wake of the authority transition that occurred after the Libyan Civil War. The Gaddafi regime had yet to be replaced and Stevens expressed concern about the lack of security in the area. He wrote, "Militias the prime power on the ground. Weak state security institutions. As a result, dicey conditions." Even more worrisome for Stevens is that he apparently knew he had been the target of militant Islamists. This was evident in his entry that said, "Islamist 'hit list' in Benghazi. Me targeted. . ."

Ambassador understood Libya better than just about any other American and he also knew that he was in a dangerous situation. It is possible, though, that he might have felt too much at home with the Libyans, given his strong local bonds and genial rapport with many Libyans. He might have believed he was in control of the situation. Even if that was the case, it's evident that he knew the risks he faced in Libya and he chose to work there anyway.

Just two days before his death, on September 9, the situation was becoming more and more overwhelming for Ambassador Stevens. He wrote, "Stressful day. Too many things going on everyone wants to bend my ear. Need to pull above the fray." Stevens was aware of the worsening conditions in the area, but he continued to believe he could handle the volatility.

On September 10, the day before his murder, Ambassador Stevens was feeling more at home in Benghazi. He wrote, "Back in Benghazi after 9 months. It's a good feeling, given all the memories." He also documented a meeting with the new team in Libya, but it is unclear whether he met with them at the Temporary Mission Facility, commonly referred to as the "consulate" or the CIA annex. He also met with 20 Libyan council members and the Mayor or Benghazi on this day as well.

Also on September 10, at least 18 hours prior to the start of the attack, al-Qaeda leader Ayman al-Zawahiri released a video in which he told his followers to attack Americans in Libya. Al-Zawahiri timed the release to coincide with the anniversary of the September 11,

2001 attacks in New York and Washington D.C. He said the attacks should be executed to avenge the drone-strike death of Abu Yahya al-Libi in Pakistan three months earlier.

Chapter 3

The Day and Night of the Attack

On September 11, 2012, nothing seemed amiss, at least during the day. Stevens wrote, "It is so nice to be back in Benghazi. Much stronger emotional connection to this place – the people but also the smaller-town feel & the moist air & green & spacious compound." He was in his element and although he knew there were significant security risks, his love for the Libyans and his desire to bring peace to the area through his ambassadorship kept him from leaving, as other diplomats had.

Ambassador Stevens met with several prominent Libyans, including Naeem Jabril, an appellate court judge; Mahmoud Mufti, a shipping company owner and Ali Akin, the Turkish Consul General. He does not indicate what was discussed during these meetings, but he does remark that Ali Akin "helped me land in Benghazi last year."

He also indicates that the day marked the "second day of PM presentation and debate. Jabril reportedly fared well. Probably also Mufti. Baja says Jabril should win. But they're worried about the MB & extremists denying him his rightful (unintelligible) or making life difficult if he wins." This last paragraph references another meeting with Fatih Baja, who is a Libyan academic who holds a PhD in Political Science. He represented the transitional Council for Benghazi and had been assuring Stevens that Libya would not follow in the footsteps of other countries whose transitional governments did not succeed.

Unfortunately, it was fairly apparent that Libya's transitional government was not succeeding and was about to collapse at the time of Stevens' death. The final paragraph in Stevens' diary says, "Bubaker Habib & Sanga, the Bgzi LES, have been very helpful. Also re-connected with Feb 17 rebel Tala & other guards from the old days. Never ending security threats. . ."

That night, according to a guard on duty, was quiet. There were no protests and nothing seemed to be out of the ordinary. However, one eyewitness indicated that militants were attempting to get a small group of people a few blocks away from the compound to begin protesting.

Ambassador Stevens had gone to his bedroom at about 9:00 p.m. local time, where he would remain until the attack began. Forty minutes later, the security guard, who was injured in the attack, said he heard "loud noises" coming from the gate at the front of the compound. He then reported he heard "gunfire and an explosion."

Only seven Americans were in the main compound when the first attack began at about 9:40 p.m., local time. Ambassador Stevens was one of the seven. Approximately 150 gunmen, some of whom were dressed in Afghan-like tunics, which is the dress preferred by Islamic militants, stormed the compound, yelling "Allahu Akbar". They were armed with a wide range of weapons, including rocket-propelled grenades (RPGs), FN F2000 assault rifles, hand grenades, mortars and diesel canisters. They even had machine guns mounted on trucks, along with other heavy artillery.

These trucks, referred to as gun trucks, blocked the streets leading to the compound. They were imprinted with the logo of Ansar al-Sharia, which is a band of militants who was known to the United

States as a group that had been working with the local government to help keep order in Benghazi.

Militants began throwing grenades over the compound wall and then followed them up with automatic gunfire and RPGs to get them into the building. This part of the attack was captured by a security camera that was currently being monitored by a Diplomatic Security agent. When he saw the large group of men storming the compound, he sent out an alert to the rest of the facility over the intercom system, warning them of the attack.

As soon as the seven Americans in the compound were notified of the attack, calls were made to the Libyan February 17 Brigade, the Tripoli Embassy, the Diplomatic Security Command Center in Washington D.C. and a United States Quick Reaction Team stationed a mile away at the CIA annex compound. Gregory Hicks, the Deputy Chief of Mission in Tripoli, received three calls from Ambassador Stevens, but Hicks did not answer the first two calls because the telephone number showing up on his caller ID was not familiar to him. He did answer the third call.

Ambassador Stevens, along with information management officer, Sean Smith, were escorted to a safe haven room by DSS special agent Scott Strickland as soon as the attack began. All other DSS agents in the compound were ordered to retrieve M4 carbines and tactical gear from another building on the property. However, when they attempted to get back into the building where Ambassador Stevens was holed up, they were forced to retreat when they encountered heavy gunfire.

Meanwhile, the militants tried to break into the safe haven but the locks proved too difficult for them to open. Instead, they dumped diesel fuel on the furniture and throughout the building. They then lit it on fire, which quickly sent smoke pouring into the safe haven room. Stevens, Strickland and Smith moved into the haven's bathroom, where they laid on the floor to avoid breathing as much of the smoke as possible. They intended to wait out the attack, but the smoke quickly became too thick for them to withstand.

The three trapped men decided they would have to vacate the safe haven to escape smoke inhalation. Strickland exited the room through an open window, but when he turned around, Smith and Stevens had not followed. Strickland went back into the room twice, attempting to locate them and bring them to safety. Unfortunately, he could not find them because the smoke obscured his vision and forced him back outside.

Strickland made his way to the roof and sent out a distress call via radio. Three other agents answered the call, arriving in an armored truck and searching the compound for Stevens and Smith. In the meantime, the alarm went off and the Regional Security Office made calls to the CIA annex compound and the Tripoli Embassy. While they were explaining the situation, the call was abruptly cut off as the attack intensified. The CIA's Global Response Staff (GRS) deployed rescue operatives, one of whom as Tyrone S. Woods.

The GRS team was briefed and on their way to the compound in their Toyota Land Cruisers by 10:05 p.m. local time. As they were preparing to launch their rescue mission, the CIA annex notified the United States of the developing situation according the proper chain of command.

The GRS team's first course of action was to secure the perimeter and search for Stevens and Smith. DSS agent David Ubben came across Smith, who was initially thought to be unconscious, but he was later declared dead. The team was unsuccessful at finding

Stevens, since the building was still filled with smoke. The team determined the situation was too dangerous to continue the search efforts and chose to make their way back to the CIA annex with Smith's body and the survivors they had picked up at the compound.

On the way back to the CIA annex, the convoy came under attack by hand grenades and an AK-47 rifle. Although their vehicle suffered two flat tires, it was able to make it back to the annex at about 11:50 p.m., local time, when the gates were closed. No one was injured in this attack, however, just after midnight the annex itself came under attack, despite the fact that Abdel-Monem Al-Hurr, the Libyan Supreme Security Committee spokesperson, assured them that the roads leading to the consulate were not only closed, but also blocked by state security officers.

The team at the annex took up defensive positions, with four agents on the roof manning and the rest positioned around the annex. Glen Doherty, who had arrived in Benghazi that evening as a reinforcement to assist in evacuating Americans from the annex to the airport, went in search of his friend, Tyrone Woods. Woods, a Navy SEAL, was one of the agents on the roof and was manning a MK46 machine gun when Doherty located him.

They spoke for a few minutes during a lull in the fighting, updating each other on their lives, but shortly thereafter, a mortar round struck Woods and fatally wounded him. Doherty attempted to retreat to a safer position, but a second mortar round hit him before he could get to safety. He died instantly. DSS Special Agent David Ubben, who had located Smith's body, was injured in the attack, suffering several broken bones along with shrapnel wounds.

Several other agents arrived on the roof to evacuate the wounded and recover the dead. At this time, a JSOC operator was viewing images from a Predator drone on a hand-held device that showed "a large element assembling" outside of the annex. The drone had been ordered to the area by the DOD's Africa Command at the CIA's request. A determination was made that everyone should be evacuated to the airport, and within minutes, they were loaded onto vehicles and on their way. During the journey, they were besieged by small arms fire, but no one sustained any further injuries.

Once the first attack was over, Libyans went into the compound and located Ambassador Stevens, who was lying on the floor, overcome by the smoke in the room. Since the only door into the room was locked, the Libyans had to pull Stevens through the window. They carried him to the complex's courtyard, where a gathering crowd cheered because he was still alive at the time.

As documented by Fahd al-Bakoush, a freelance videographer, Stevens was then taken to the Benghazi Medical Center by car, since no ambulances were available to take him. Dr. Ziad Abu Zeid gave Stevens CPR for 90 minutes upon his arrival at the Ansar Al-Sharia militia-controlled hospital. However, the resuscitation efforts failed and Stevens was declared dead. The cause of death was determined to be asphyxiation by smoke inhalation, as Stevens suffered no other injuries.

It remains unknown as to who brought Stevens to the hospital, just as it remains a mystery as to who transported his body to the airport and delivered it to the United States. There have been reports that two JSOC operators were in the area when the attacks occurred and that they ventured out of their safe house, retrieved Stevens' body from the hospital and took it to the airport.

At 6:07 Eastern Time, the State Department's Operations Center emailed the Pentagon, White House, FBI and other federal agencies apprising them that the militia group Ansar al-Sharia was claiming responsibility for the attack on its social media pages. About four hours later, Secretary of State Hillary Clinton issued a formal statement confirming the death of a state official in Benghazi. This statement, which was released by the media at 10:32, referenced the anti-Muslim video that purportedly sparked the attack.

Chapter 4

Libyan Response

Ambassador Stevens greatly loved the Libyan people and that affection was returned after his death, when demonstrations sprung up around the region protesting the violence that ended his life. In addition, the Libyan Prime Minister Mustafa Abushagur condemned the attack, stating: "While strongly condemning any attempt to abuse the person of Muhammad, or an insult to our holy places and prejudice against the faith, we reject and strongly condemn the use of force to terrorize innocent people and the killing of innocent people. We apologize to the United States, the people and to the whole world for what happened. We confirm that no-one will escape punishment and questioning."

The Libyan President, Mohamed Yousef el-Magariaf announced on September 16 that the country's investigation determined the attack on the consulate had been months in the planning. He disputed the United States' initial claim that the attack had been the result of a riot that had gotten out of hand.

Ten days after the attack, approximately 30,000 Libyans marched through Benghazi, seeking to put a stop to the armed militias that had arisen during Colonel Gaddafi's reign. These militias had continued to terrorize Libyans and were a constant menace to the transitional government. A faction of these protestors even stormed militia headquarters, including that of the Ansar al-Sharia, which had claimed responsibility for the attack on the consulate that killed Ambassador Stevens.

In response to the uprising against the militias, the Libyan government formed a "National Mobile Force" to evict illegal groups from the country. On September 23, Magariaf announced that all militias were to disband or come under control of the government within 48 hours. In addition, it became illegal to carry weapons in public and checkpoints were established to enforce this law.

One day later, the government raided a defunct military base that was being used by an infantry militia. Following this raid, militias across the country began surrendering to the government. By September 29th, a large number of militia members had turned in their weapons to the government.

Chapter 5

United States Response

The first known public response to the Benghazi attacks was Hillary Clinton's statement that confirmed the death of a state official in an attack on the Benghazi U.S. consulate. This was released to the media at 10:32 p.m. Eastern Time. In the statement, Clinton wrote: "Some have sought to justify this vicious behavior as a response to inflammatory material posted on the Internet. The United States deplores any intentional effort to denigrate the religious beliefs of others. Our commitment to religious tolerance goes back to the very beginning of our nation. But let me be clear: There is never any justification for violent acts of this kind.

September 12

Clinton followed up this response with a second statement released on September 12 confirming the deaths of four U.S. officials in the attacks on Benghazi instead of just one. In this statement, she wrote: "All the Americans we lost in yesterday's attacks made the ultimate sacrifice. We condemn this vicious and violent attack that took their lives, which they had committed to helping the Libyan people reach for a better future."

Later that same day, Clinton gave a speech at the State Department, in which she condemned the attack and hailed the victims as heroes. In this speech, she once again referenced the anti-Muslim video as the impetus for the attacks: "Some have sought to justify this vicious behavior, along with the protest that took place at our Embassy in Cairo yesterday, as a response to inflammatory material posted on the Internet. America's commitment to religious tolerance goes back to the very beginning of our nation. But let me be clear – there is no justification for this, none.

U.S. president Barack Obama also issued a statement on September 12 that denounced the attacks as "outrageous." He also said: "Since our founding, the United States has been a nation that respects all faiths. We reject all efforts to denigrate the religious beliefs of others. No acts of terror will ever shake the resolve of this great nation, alter that character, or eclipse the light of the values that we stand for. Today we mourn four more Americans who represent the very best of the United States of America. We will not waver in our commitment to see that justice is done for this terrible act. And make no mistake, justice will be done.

The president ordered an increase in security at all U.S. facilities worldwide and he deployed a 50-member Marine Fast team to Libya to add more security there. He gave the FBI the responsibility of investigating the events that occurred prior to, during and after the attack. He also asked the FBI to determine whether or not the attacks were planned.

Obama later said that he purposely did not use the word "terrorism" in his condemnation of the acts because "it's too early to know exactly how this came about." In an interview for "60 Minutes", which he taped after his speech, the show's host, Steve Kroft asked Obama how the attack could be construed as an impulsive "mob action" if the people who perpetuated the attack were "very heavily armed." Obama states, "We're still investigating," but he also admits, "folks involved in this . . . were looking to target Americans from the start."

Senior administration officials also indicated at a later briefing that it is "too early to say who they were" and their affiliation, even though they both characterized the attackers as "extremists" during the briefing. They also responded to a question about whether or not the attack had been related to an anti-Muslim video with "We just don't know."

White House Press Secretary Jay Carney repeated the refrain during a press briefing on the way to Las Vegas. He was asked, "Does the White House believe that the attack in Benghazi was planned and premeditated." His response was, "It's too early for us to make that judgment. I think — I know that this is being investigated, and we're working with the Libyan government to investigate the incident. So I would not want to speculate on that at this time."

In contrast to the White House's ambiguous statements, Libya's deputy ambassador to London, Ahmad Jibril, who met with Ambassador Stevens on the day of his death, told the BBC that the militant group Ansar al-Sharia was responsible for the attack. Ansar al-Sharia did not confirm or deny that statement, but did say that it "didn't participate as a sole entity."

By the end of the day, September 12, there was widespread speculation that "the Benghazi attack may have been planned in advance," as was reported first by Reuters that evening. The name "Ansar al-Sharia" is mentioned as having possibly been involved. The report also quoted an unnamed U.S. official that said the attack ". . .bears the hallmarks of an organized attack." An email from Beth Jones, the acting secretary of state for the Near East, seems to confirm this suspicion: "[T]he group that conducted the attacks, Ansar al-Sharia, is affiliated with Islamic extremists."

According to reports, the United States also sent two destroyers to the coast of Libya, both of which were equipped with Tomahawk cruise missiles. In addition, UAVs were ordered to perform fly-overs over Libya.

September 13

Secretary of State Hillary Clinton met with Ali Suleiman Aujali, the Libyan Ambassador to the United States at a State Department event marking the end of Ramadan. At the meeting, Ambassador Aujali apologized to Clinton for what he referred to as "this terrorist attack which took place against the American consulate in Libya." Clinton continued to condemn the attack as a response to the anti-Muslim video, even though she did say there is "never any justification for violent acts of this kind."

State Department spokeswoman Victoria Nuland was asked at the daily press briefing if the attack on Benghazi was "purely spontaneous or was premeditated by militants?" Her only response was to reiterate the administration did not want to "jump to conclusions." She said the State Department was being very cautious about naming perpetrators and speculating on their motivations until they had a chance to fully investigate the situation. She also referenced the "disgusting video as something that has been motivating" but she repeated Clinton's words that there is never an excuse to use violence of this nature.

That day, Clinton also held a meeting with Moroccan Foreign Minister Saad0Eddine Al-Othmani, who used the opportunity to condemn the anti-Muslim video and the violence it spawned. She said, "Islam, like other religions, respects the fundamental dignity of human beings, and it is a violation of that fundamental dignity to wage attacks on innocents. As long as there are those who are willing to shed blood and take innocent life in the name of religion, the name of God, the world will never know a true and lasting peace."

President Obama, who was attending a campaign event in Colorado, again referred to the attack as an "act of terror." He repeated his remarks from the day before, saying, "I want people around the world to hear me: To all those who would do us harm, no act of terror will go unpunished."

A CNN report that evening cited anonymous state department officials that said that the event in Benghazi was a "clearly planned military-type attack" that had nothing to do with the anti-Muslim video. The unnamed senior official said, "It was not an innocent mob. The video or 9/11 made a handy excuse and could be fortuitous from their perspective."

September 14

At a ceremony at Andrews Air Force Base to receive the remains of the victims of the Benghazi attack, Clinton said that she received a letter from the Palestine Authority president lauding Stevens and "deploring – and I quote – 'an act of ugly terror.'" Clinton did not refer to the event as a terrorist attack and neither did President Obama.

State Department spokeswoman Nuland told the media at the daily press briefing that the department would no longer be answering questions about the attack in Benghazi. She said, "It is now something that you need to talk to the FBI about, not to us about, because it's their investigation."

White House Press Secretary Carney, at a White House press briefing, referenced the CNN report indicating the attack was preplanned and denied its validity. He said, "I have seen that report, and the story is absolutely wrong. We were not aware of any actionable intelligence indicating that an attack on the U.S. mission in Benghazi was planned or imminent. That report is false."

Carney was notified during the briefing that Pentagon officials told Congressional members during a closed-door meeting that the attack on Benghazi was preplanned. Carney informed the attendees that the attack was still being investigated but at the time "did not have concrete evidence to suggest that this was not in reaction to the film." He also said, "There was no intelligence that in any way could have been acted on to prevent these attacks . . . We have no information to suggest that it was a preplanned attack. The unrest we have seen around the region has been in reaction to a video that Muslims, many Muslims find offensive. And while the violence is reprehensible and unjustified, it is not a reaction to the 9/11 anniversary that we know of, or to U.S. policy."

Roll Call, a Capitol Hill newspaper, reported that at a meeting between Defense Secretary Leon Panetta and the Senate Armed Services Committee, both Democrats and Republicans got the impression that the attack on Benghazi was a planned terrorist attack. Armed Services Chairman Carl Levin said, "I think it was a planned, premeditated attack" but he did not know who was responsible for the act. Senator John McCain echoed Levin's opinion, stating "People don't go to demonstrate and carry RPGs and automatic weapons . . . This was not a 'mob' action [or] a group of protesters."

September 15

In his weekly address, Obama mentions the Benghazi attack, but does not call it an act of terror, terrorism or the work of extremists.

He does talk about the anti-Muslim video and "every angry mob" that it incited in areas of the Middle East.

September 16

On CBS's "Face the Nation", Libya President Mohamed Magariaf said that the Benghazi attack was planned several months in advance. However, U.S. ambassador to the United Nations, Susan Rice told Bob Schieffer of CBS News: "We do not have information at present that leads us to conclude that this was premeditated or preplanned." She also said the event started "spontaneously . . . as a reaction to what had transpired some hours earlier in Cairo."

She did state that "it's clear that there were extremist elements that joined in and escalated the violence. Whether they were al Qaeda affiliates, whether they were Libyan-based extremists or al Qaeda itself I think is one of the things we'll have to determine."

Rice's comments, though, were from a CIA report that was heavily revised by the State Department before she delivered them. Originally, the report said, "We do know that Islamic extremists with ties to Al-Qaeda participated in the attack," and that "[i]nitial press reports linked the attack to Ansar al-Sharia." All references to Ansar al-Sharia and al-Qaeda were redacted from the report before it was passed on to Rice. All other drafts of the report included the notion that the attack began "spontaneously" in response to the protest in Cairo.

Magariaf continued to make the circuit of news programs that day, giving an interview to NPR during which he said, "The idea that this criminal and cowardly act was a spontaneous protest that just spun out of control is completely unfounded and preposterous. We firmly believe that this was a precalculated, preplanned attack that was carried out specifically to attack the U.S. consulate."

September 17

State Department Spokeswoman Nuland defended Rice's comments made on "Face the Nation" and four other Sunday news programs the day before. Nuland said, "The comments that Ambassador Rice made accurately reflect our government's initial assessment." Nuland made sure to emphasize "initial assessment," repeating it three times during her defense of Rice's statements.

September 18

President Obama appeared on "The Late Show with David Letterman" and when questioned about the attack on Benghazi, he stated, "Here's what happened." He went on to talk about the anti-Muslim video and the impact it had on people in the region. He said, "Extremists and terrorists used this as an excuse to attack a variety of our embassies, including the consulate in Libya." He also repeated Clinton's earlier refrain, stating: "As offensive as this video was and, obviously, we've denounced it and the United States government had nothing to do with it. That's never an excuse for violence."

White House spokesman Carney, in response to a question regarding Magariaf's claim that the video was not the cause of the attack, said that Obama "would rather wait" for the results of the investigation before commenting on those remarks. He went on to say, "But at this time, as Ambassador Rice said and as I said, our understanding and our belief based on the information we have is it was the video that caused the unrest in Cairo, and the video and the unrest in Cairo that helped – the precipitated some of the unrest in Benghazi and elsewhere."

Following a meeting with Mexican Secretary of Foreign Relations Patricia Espinosa, Clinton was asked by reporters if Magariaf is wrong that the attack was preplanned. Clinton responded, "The Office of the Director of National Intelligence has said we had no actionable intelligence that an attack on our post in Benghazi was planned or imminent." She did not directly answer whether or not Magariaf is wrong.

September 19

National Counterterrorism director Matt Olsen addressed a Senate subcommittee, stating that the four State Department Officials in Benghazi "were killed in the course of a terrorist attack on the embassy . . . The best information we have now, the facts that we have now, indicate that this was an opportunist attack on our embassy. The attack began and evolved and escalated over several hours. . . .[I]t appears that individuals who were certainly well armed seized on the opportunity presented as the events unfolded. . . ." This marks the first occasion that anyone affiliated with the administration labeled the event a "terrorist attack." However, he also said that there was no "specific evidence of significant advanced planning or coordination for this attack."

State Department spokeswoman Nuland was asked at a State Department briefing if she would characterize the attack as a "terrorist attack"? Nuland replied, "Well, I didn't get a chance to see the whole testimony that was given by Matt Olsen of the NCTC, but obviously we stand by comments made by our intelligence community who has first responsibility for evaluating the intelligence and what they believe that we are seeing."

White House spokesman Carney still refused to all it a "terrorist attack". During the White House press briefing for the day, he said, "Based on the information we had at the time – we have now, we do not yet have indication that it was preplanned or premeditated.

There's an active investigation. If that active investigation produces facts that lead to a different conclusion, we will make clear that that's where the investigation has led."

September 20

Nine days after the attack that killed Ambassador Stevens and four other Americans, White House spokesman Carney called the attack a "terrorist attack" during a White House press briefing when a reporter asked how the administration was classifying the event. However, he also said the administration has no evidence that it was "a significantly preplanned attack." He continues to place blame for the Benghazi incident on the anti-Muslim video, stating, ". . .this was the result of opportunism, taking advantage of and exploiting what was happening as a result of reaction to the video that was found to be offensive."

At a town hall meeting, Obama reiterated this theory, stating that "extremists" took advantage of the "natural protests" in response to the anti-Muslim video. He does not refer to the attack as a "terrorist attack," but he does say the investigation was still underway: "Well, we're still doing an investigation, and there are going to be different circumstances in different countries. And so I don't want to speak to something until we have all the information."

September 21

Prior to a meeting with Pakistani Foreign Minister Hina Rabbani Khar, Clinton told reporters that the Benghazi incident was in fact a "terrorist attack." This was the first time she used those words in connection with the events that had occurred ten days earlier. She said, "Yesterday afternoon when I briefed the Congress, I made it clear that keeping our people everywhere in the world safe is our top priority. What happened in Benghazi was a terrorist attack, and we will not rest until we have tracked down and brought to justice the terrorists who murdered four Americans."

September 24

In a meeting with Libyan President Magariaf, Clinton again calls the attack on Benghazi a "terrorist assault." She said, "As we all know, the United States lost a great ambassador and the Libyan people lost a true friend when Chris Stevens and three other Americans were killed in the terrorist assault on our consulate in Benghazi."

Obama, though, refuses to call the event a terrorist attack while appearing on "The View". Co-Host Joy Behar asked the president whether the attack in Libya was a terrorist act or a violent response to the anti-Muslim video. Obama responded, "Well, we're still doing an investigation. There's no doubt that the kind of weapons that were used, the ongoing assault, that it wasn't just a mob action. Now, we don't have all the information yet, so we're still gathering it. But what's clear is that around the world, there's still a lot of threats out there."

September 26

When questioned about why the president had not called the Benghazi attack a terrorist attack during an Air Force One press briefing, White House spokesman Carney said, "The president – our position is, as reflected by the NCTC director, that it was a terrorist attack. It is, I think by definition, a terrorist attack when there is a prolonged assault on an embassy with weapons. . . . So, let's be clear, it was a terrorist attack and it was an inexcusable attack."

In an interview with Al Jazeera, Deputy Secretary of State William Burns is questioned as to whether or not he agrees with Libyan president Magariaf when he says the attack on Benghazi was premeditated and had nothing to do with the anti-Muslim film. He said, "It's clear that the attack which took the lives of Chris Stevens and three other colleagues was clearly choreographed and directed and involved a fair amount of firepower, but exactly what kind of planning went into that and how it emerged on that awful night, we just don't know right now. But I'm confident we'll get to the bottom of it."

September 27

During a press briefing, Defense Secretary Leon Panetta said the Benghazi incident was a terrorist attack but did not specify when he reached that conclusion. He continued, "It took a while to really get some of the feedback from what exactly happened at that location. As we determined the details of what took place there, and how the attack took place, that it became clear that there were terrorists who had planned the attack."

At that same briefing, Army General Martin E. Dempsey, Chairman of the Joint Chiefs of Staff talked about what the United States knew about the attack before it happened. He said there was "a thread of intelligence reporting that groups in . . . eastern Libya were seeking to coalesce, but there wasn't anything specific and certainly not a specific threat to the consulate that I'm aware of."

White House spokesman Carney is questioned once again about why the president has chosen not to refer to the attack as a terrorist attack. Carney replied, "the president's position [is] that this was a terrorist attack."

Later that day, on "Anderson Cooper 360 Degrees," former Homeland Security adviser under President George W. Bush, Fran Townsend said that the administration knew it was a terrorist attack from the start. She said, "The law enforcement source who said to me, from day one we had known that this was a terrorist attack."

September 28

Director of National Intelligence spokesman Shawn Turner released a statement that said the office's position on the incident in Benghazi evolved from believing it was a spontaneous mob event to an organized, planned terrorist attack. The statement said in part, "In the immediate aftermath, there was information that led us to assess that the attack began spontaneously following protests earlier that day at our embassy in Cairo. . . .As we learned more about the attack, we revised our initial assessment to reflect new information indicating that is was a deliberate and organized terrorist attack carried out by extremists. It remains unclear if any group or person exercised overall command and control of the attack and if extremist group leaders directed their members to participate."

October 2

At a press briefing in Nevada, White House spokesman Carney said, "At every step of the way, the administration has based its public statements on the best assessments that were provided by the intelligence community. As the intelligence community learned more information they updated Congress and the American people on it."

Following a meeting with Kazakhstan Foreign Minister Erlan Idrissov, Clinton addressed reporters, stating, "There are continuing questions about what exactly happened in Benghazi that night three weeks ago. And we will not rest until we answer those questions and until we track down the terrorists who killed our people."

October 4

FBI investigators were finally allowed to investigate the scene of the attack. Until then, the Annex and the consulate could not be secured by either American or Libyan authorities. The Obama administration earmarked $8 million dollars to establish an elite Libyan commando force to help stabilize the area.

October 9

Senior State Department officials release information to the public stating that there were no protests before the start of the attack in Benghazi, which was in direct contrast to the statements made by the administration and its officials since the night of the attack. A senior official said, "everything is calm at 8:30 p.m., (Libya time)" when Stevens said goodbye to a visitor outside of the consulate. The ambassador went to his bedroom at 9:00 p.m. and the silence was broken at 9:40 p.m. when "loud noises" and "gunfire and an explosion" were heard.

Another official said it was "not our conclusion" that the attack began spontaneously in response to the anti-Muslim film. He also indicated that "there was no actionable intelligence of any planned or imminent attack."

October 10

At a press briefing, White House spokesman Carney is questioned about why the president and other administration officials said the anti-Muslim film was the impetus for the attack when the State Department released a statement saying it had "never concluded that the assault in Benghazi was part of a protest on the anti-

Muslim film"? Carney responded, "Again, from the beginning, we have provided information based on the facts that we knew as they became available, based on assessments by the intelligence community – not opinions – assessments by the IC, by the intelligence community. And we have been clear all along that this was an ongoing investigation, that as more facts became available we would make you aware of them as appropriate, and we've done that."

Under Secretary for Management Patrick Kennedy was asked following his testimony before a House committee how the State Department could have better released information concerning the Benghazi attack? Kennedy replied, "[T]his is obviously an incredibly complicated situation. We've always made it clear from the very beginning that we are giving out the best information we have at the time we are giving it out."

State Department memos are released by the House Committee on Oversight and Government Reform that show additional security was requested in Libya. The State Department official who denied those requests, Charlene Lamb, testified that the State Department had been in the process of training local Libyans for the past 12 months so additional U.S. security personnel were not necessary. She said, "We had the correct number of assets in Benghazi on the night of 9/11."

Other officials remembered the situation differently. Eric Nordstrom, the top regional security officer in Libya prior to the attack said, "All of us at post were in sync that we wanted these resources."

October 15

In an interview on CNN, when asked why the administration said the attack was sparked by the anti-Muslim video despite the fact that the State Department hadn't come to that conclusion, Clinton said, "In the wake of an attack like this in the fog of war, there's always going to be confusion, and I think it is absolutely fair to say that everyone had the same intelligence. Everyone who spoke tried to give the information they had. As time has gone on, the information has changed, we've gotten more detail, but that's not surprising. That always happens."

The New York Times also came out with a report on this day that said the attack on Benghazi occurred "without any warning or protest," but "Libyans who witnessed the assault and know the attackers" have said it was "in retaliation for the video."

October 24

Using information from three State Department emails originating from the Operations Center, Reuters released a report that the White House, Pentagon and other federal agencies knew within two hours of the start of the Benghazi attack that Ansar al-Sharia had "claimed credit" for it. One email said, "Embassy Tripoli reports group claimed responsibility on Facebook and Twitter and has called for an attack on Embassy Tripoli." In addition, the report also said, "Intelligence experts caution that initial reports from the scene of any attack or disaster are often inaccurate."

In response to the Reuter's article, Clinton warned the press that they should not rely on information gleaned from leaked emails because "cherry-picking one story here or one document there" can lead to misinformation. She also said, "The independent Accountability Review Board is already hard at work looking into everything – not cherry-picking one story here or one document there – but looking at everything, which I highly recommend as the appropriate approach to something as complex as an attack like this. Posting something on Facebook is not in and of itself evidence, and I think it just underscores how fluid the reporting was at the time and continued for some time to be."

White House spokesman Carney contradicted the Reuters' report altogether, stating, "Within a few hours" of the attack Ansar al-Sharia "claimed that it had not been responsible." He said, "Neither [report] should be taken as fact – that's why there's an investigation underway."

May 8, 2013

Representative Trey Gowdy, at a House Committee on Oversight and Government Reform hearing, read parts of a September 12, 2012 email composed by Acting Assistant Secretary of State for the Near East Beth Jones. She wrote, "I spoke to the Libyan ambassador and emphasized the importance of Libyan leaders to continue to make strong statements, " and "When he said his government suspected that former Qaddafi regime elements carried out the attack, I told him that the group that conducted the attacks, Ansar al-Sharia, is affiliated with Islamic extremists."

According to Gowdy, the email was distributed to several top State Department officials, one of whom was Under Secretary for Management Patrick Kennedy. The full emails were not released and Speaker of the House John Boehner indicated that the State Department did not permit the House to retain a copy.

May 15, 2013

100 pages of emails concerning the CIA's original talking points that were written for the House Permanent Select Committee on

Intelligence were released. These were the statements the State Department revised before U.S. Ambassador to the United Nations Susan Rice appeared on five Sunday news shows on September 16. The emails prove there were extensive revisions made before she was given the talking points to use.

Chapter 6

Investigations

Several investigations were launched in the aftermath of the Benghazi attacks, many of which are still ongoing. Neither the FBI nor the CIA has claimed responsibility for the incident, even though some groups believe they should. Three investigations have been closed: one by the State Committee, one by the Governmental Affairs Committee and one by the State Department Accountability Review Board.

Ongoing Investigations

The FBI investigation into the events that occurred in Benghazi on September 11, 2012 is still ongoing and remains unresolved. Although the FBI released photos of potential suspects in May, 2013, no arrests have been forthcoming.

A second investigation is still underway by the Five-House Committee, which is made up of representatives from five governmental branches, including Foreign Affairs, Armed Services, Judiciary, Intelligence and Oversight of Government Reform. An interim report into their findings was released on April 23, 2013. The report indicated:

- White House and State Department officials revised CIA talking points to protect the State Department in the days following the incident.
- The talking point revisions were not made to keep sensitive and classified information from reaching the public. Such concerns were not addressed in any email exchanges.

- The decision to reduce security forces in Benghazi was made at the highest level, which included Secretary of State Clinton. This is contrary to her testimony to the House Foreign Affairs Committee.

The Five-House Committee also decided that more review would be required in order to determine who did not properly handle the requests for additional security.

Closed Investigations

The State Department Accountability Review Board was required to investigate the facts surrounding the Benghazi attack by the Omnibus and Antiterrorism Act of 1986. Five members served on the board, including Ambassador Thomas R. Pickering, who served as Chairman; Admiral Michael Mullen, who served as Vice Chairman and three Intelligence Community representatives, Richard Scninnick, Hugh Turner and Catherine Bertini.

The board concluded:

1. The attack on Benghazi was related to a lack of security. Small arms, machine guns, RPGs, grenades, arson and mortars were all used against U.S. personnel at both the Annex and the consulate. In addition, force was used as U.S. personnel attempted to travel between the two areas. The terrorists who participate in the event are solely responsible for the deaths of four Americans, the injuries of Americans and the damage to U.S. facilities and properties. The Board did not find any evidence of protests prior to the attacks.
2. Both bureaus of the State Department failed to provide both leadership and management that resulted inadequate security levels in Benghazi. The report indicated that the

consulate was greatly understaffed when the attack occurred.

The local Benghazi security team was fairly inexperienced, as all assignments were only on the job about 40 days. This meant that they did not have as much knowledge or continuity in protecting the consulate.

In the months leading up to the attack and on the day of the attack, Benghazi security was minimal at best. Although there were repeated requests to Washington asking for more security detail, they were largely ignored by the State Department. In addition, the Benghazi consulate failed to meet the Overseas Security Policy Board (OSPB) standards. There wasn't enough security equipment or personnel even though there had been physical upgrades performed earlier in 2012.

Since Washington and Embassy Tripoli had not responded to the requests for more security, the consulate had to rely on the Libyan February 17 Martyrs' Brigade, the members of which did not have adequate training. In fact, they frequently did not have weapons either.

Ambassador Stevens and Benghazi-based DS agents held meetings at the compound on September 11, 2012, despite the presence of significant threats and the anniversary of the September 11 terrorist attacks on New York and Washington D.C.

3. On the night of the attack, the Libyan February 17 Martyrs' Brigade and the BML did not respond appropriately to the attack. However, the Libyan Government did assist Americans with evacuation.

The Board found that the U.S. personnel on the ground in Benghazi acted with courage and were willing to protect the lives of everyone in the area. Although the interagency timing was appropriate, they were not given enough advance warning to be of any real help.

4. There was no prior warning of the attack.
5. The two bureaus of the State Department demonstrated a lack of management and leadership abilities; however, the Board was unable to name any one U.S. government employee who had not performed his or her duty on that day.

As a result of their investigation, the Board suggested that improvements be made in the following areas:

- Staffing High Risk
- Training and Awareness
- High Threat Posts
- Overarching Security Considerations
- Intelligence and Threat Analysis
- Security and Fire Safety Equipment
- Personnel Accountability

In mid-October, 2012, Joe Lieberman, Homeland Security Chairman, and Susan Collins, ranking member of the Governmental Affairs Committee conducted an investigation on the attack in Benghazi. Their findings were released on December 31, 2012. They found that in the months leading up to the September 11 attack on Benghazi there was a high risk for terrorist attacks in the region. They also found that the State Department did not provide adequate security to maintain the Benghazi mission's integrity.

On January 18, 2013, Republican Representative Frank Wolf introduced a bill to establish a committee that would investigate the Benghazi attack and issue a report. As of May 9, 2013, the bill had two-thirds of the vote in the Republican-led House of Representatives. 700 special operations veterans and Special Operations OPSEC are in full support of the measure.

Non-Governmental Investigations

Former Navy SEAL Brandon Webb and Army Ranger Jack Murphy published an e-book titled "Benghazi: The Definitive Report" in February, 2013. The book gives a minute-by-minute account of the events that occurred on September 11, 2012 based on statements from confidential sources that lived through the experience. It details both the first attack on the consulate and the subsequent attack on the CIA annex. It also discusses JSOC operations in Libya in the months leading up to the attack. According to the authors, the reports correctly predicted the Benghazi attack.

Murphy and Webb said that in the summer before the attack, members of al-Qaeda were targets by Libyan militia groups. They were mostly targeting members related to Yasin al-Suri in an attempt to lure al-Suri in the open. This strategy was to give the JSOC an opportunity to kill or capture him. Murphy surmised that al-Suri was a CIA informant. Moreover, both authors believe the attack in Benghazi was directly related to these operations due to the fact that they threatened militant groups with al-Qaeda ties, such as Ansar al-Sharia.

In addition, the authors believe that the National Security advisor to the President John O. Brennen, Under Secretary of Defense for Intelligence Michael G. Vikers and Director of National Intelligence James Clapper conducted these clandestine operations. It is their theory that neither the CIA nor the State Department knew about these plans and that is the reason they did not attempt to shield themselves from the resulting backlash.

Murphy further speculates that two members of the secret operations team recovered Ambassador Steven's remains from the Ansar al-Sharia hospital in August, 2013. He believes they were in Libya to carry out assassinations of Islamic extremists in an attempt to avoid the kind of violence that broke out in Iraq in 2007.

Stephen Hayes, a reporter for *The Weekly Standard,* issued a report on May 2, 2013 that claimed new evidence had surfaced indicating senior Obama administration officials purposefully released misleading information to the public concerning the Benghazi attack and the events that occurred in the intervening days. He referenced the revisions made to the CIA's talking points that Susan Rice used to discuss the event on Sunday news programs.

ABC News correspondent Jonathan Karl released a report on May 10, 2013 that said he discovered edited drafts of the emails originally written by the CIA to the versions Rice eventually referenced. He said there were 12 variations to the original emails. Karl appeared on ABC News' "This Week" on May 12, where he claimed that CIA Director David Patraeus advocated the revision of the talking points because they were useless. He said, "I would just as soon as not use them, but it's their (the White House's) call."

Kathleen Johnston and Drew Griffin of CNN reported in August, 2013 that on the night of the Benghazi attack, dozens of CIA operatives were already stationed in the area. Their sources told them that there were 35 agents in Benghazi that night, 21 of whom were present in the annex building during the second attack. They indicated that the CIA had taken major steps to keep their presence under wraps. In fact, some survivors were administered polygraph tests to make sure they did not talk to the media or to Congress.

According to the sources, these tactics were meant to intimidate the agents and that if anyone was found to have leaked any information, his or her career would be over. Former CIA agent Robert Baer said the polygraph tests were not a frequent occurrence. Further, the report claimed that the State Department and the CIA were in the process of arming Syrian rebels with missiles that were then in Libya.

Chapter 7

Conclusion

More than a year after the attack in Benghazi, nothing is resolved. There are still many questions as to what the U.S. government knew prior to the attacks, why it didn't respond to calls for more security and why it continued to claim the attack was the result of an anti-Muslim video when it was clear it was a planned terrorist attack.

The ongoing FBI and Five-House Committee investigations are still trying to determine exactly what happened and what the U.S. response should have been. Moreover, it is still not yet known whether or not the CIA was an active participant in the events leading up to the attack. No one has been arrested as of yet and it is unclear whether anyone will ever be held responsible.

In any case, the attack in Benghazi and the apparent purposeful misinformation following it have put the Obama administration under intense scrutiny by the media and American public. What is certain, though, is that not enough attention was given to the anniversary of 9/11. That oversight, when combined with a deliberate reduction in security in an extremely volatile part of the world, led to the deaths of four Americans who, due to repeated security threats, should never been in the area in the first place.

Sources:

http://en.wikipedia.org/wiki/2012_Benghazi_attack

http://www.washingtontimes.com/specials/benghazi-attack-and-scandal/

http://www.state.gov/documents/organization/202446.pdf

http://oversight.house.gov/wp-content/uploads/2013/04/Libya-Progress-Report-Final-1.pdf

http://www.rememberingchrisstevens.com/

http://sofrep.com/22460/ambassador-chris-stevens-benghazi-diary/#prettyPhoto

http://en.wikipedia.org/wiki/2012_Benghazi_attack#Glen_Doherty

http://www.factcheck.org/2012/10/benghazi-timeline/